A Common Rule
for Monastics

"A rule in the spiritual life is to create a space
where God's jealous love can reach us, heal us,
transform us, and guide us to freedom ...."
Henri J. M. Nouwen

2nd Edition

ISBN: 1726219828
ISBN-13: 978-1726219822

Other tools used by this Community:

Reclaiming Eden
Reclaiming Your Soul
Holy Week Prayer Book
Christmas Season Prayer Book
Living Waters from the Well

CONTENTS

INTRODUCTION

The idea for this Common Rule grew out of the realization that, over time, too many of us have become human *doings,* and have forgotten that we are actually supposed to be human *beings* first.

We live in a "doing" society today that moves fast, has many things, and fails to encourage people to connect deeply with each other – all of which tends to erode our moral foundation and the sense of who we really are as a people. We sometimes seem lost, but are too busy to realize it, or even care about it. We fill the voids within our souls with things and activities which provide us the alibis we need to avoid a face-to-face encounter with our own hearts. The busy life has become our habit, our excuse to escape the encounter we need to really live.

So, from within our monastic community, we pause for a while and re-examine *what it means to be a human being at the most basic levels.* What are the roots that tie us to life and living? What can provide the basis for knowing ourselves and understanding how we fit into this world, without succumbing to its illusion? What gives us the strength and bearing to be who we are truly made to be, thereby fulfilling the deep-seated desire in each of us to reach our full potential?

The pieces of this puzzle are scattered over the pages of time, written in many places throughout the world. They appear again and again, however, like a perennial flower in the gardens of both the East and West. They are the voices of prophets, sages, and mystics, beckoning us to join in the cosmic dance of love; an invitation that never ends, like love itself. "Come! Follow me!" Where else can we go for the truth but to the truth-givers?

The pages of this document emerge as an invitation – a call to first understand who we are as human *beings*, and then to extend that knowledge out into the world in our own unique ways, serving as models of what life could be. The offering is a life of seeing deeply, living deeply, and loving deeply – a life that values relationships more than things, and ensures the dignity and respect of *all* persons, helping each other discover the wonders of life.

While this booklet is designed for the members of the Community of the Gospel, the companion book, *Living Waters from the Well,* can be used by anyone seeking a foundation for a loving, spiritually-based life. Perhaps these books can contribute to the much-needed stability and sense of "being" in this fast-paced, hectic world that sometimes seems a little crazy.

Take the words of this Rule and discover what they mean for you. Be in the world but know where your roots grow best – in the loving Presence of your Creator as found in many places, including the far corners of your heart.

Br Daniel-Joseph Schroeder, Founder
Community of the Gospel
June 2018

1. GOD AND US

1. God is love, and God loves us
unconditionally. (1 John 4:8, 16) (Romans 8:38-39)
God's relationship with us
began long before we were born:
"Before I formed you
in your mother's womb,
I knew you." (Jeremiah 1:5)

2. God breathed into us
the Divine image
which included a strong desire
to be in unity with each other
and with creation. (Genesis 1:26, 27; 2:7)
From this we have a strong desire
to find God. (Psalm 63:1-8)

3. But we often look for God
in the wrong places.
We seek the wrong connections
and false relationships
with things or ideas.
We may believe that God
is in some far-off place,
a throne in the skies,
way beyond our reach.

4. But we are mistaken,
because God is closer,
much closer.
Truly, God abides in us,
and we abide in God.   (1 John 4:16)
God has made us into a temple
where God is intimate with our soul.
We belong to God.   (1 Corinth. 3:16-17)

5. God is not to be feared,
as there is no fear in love.   (1 John 4:18)
God's love endures forever,
and nothing can come between us
and God's love for us – nothing.   (Rom. 8:38-39)
It has always been this way,
and will always be.

6. To prove this love,
and to teach us how
to love one another,
God sent us the Son, Jesus.
Not to condemn the world,   (John 3:16)
but to save it by bringing
God's kingdom to earth.
How could God not visit what is loved?

7. To know Jesus is to know God.
To know ourselves   (John 14:7-11)
we need to imitate Jesus.
Follow his word, live his way,
forgive, share, embrace, smile, pray,
and love.
Even a small act of love
for another person,
or for a creature,
or for nature,
reveals to us what God is like.

8. Some days the distance
between us and God
may seem a very long way.
But this is our perception, not God's.
Each new moment brings an invitation
to renew our relationship with God.
Watch for signs – in the dawning sun,
in a cloud,
in a breeze,
in a quiet day,
in the face of the next person
we meet in our life.
We glorify God by
becoming who we were made to be.
Not what others think we should be –
but who God made us to be deep inside.

9. Faith in God doesn't mean
that we believe God exists.
Faith in God means that we trust
that God loves us.
Believing in God comes from the head.
This doesn't really change us much.
Having faith in God comes from the heart.
This can lead to big changes in our lives.

10. "In God We Trust"
It's on all our money.
"In God We Trust"
It's on the walls of our Congress.
"In God We Trust"
What would our world be like
if we really did trust God?

11. We seek to love the Lord God
with all our heart,
and with all our mind,
and with all our soul;
and to love our neighbor
as ourselves.
For doing something for
the least of any is doing it for God.
Walk with gratitude, hope, and joy,
for these are the fruits of the Spirit.

2. JESUS AND US

1. God so loved the world   (John 3:16)
that He sent His only begotten Son to us
so that we could learn
how to live with each other
and with all of creation.
He was sent to teach us,
to heal us,
and show us love.
He was God's free gift to us –
not to be earned, but to be accepted.

2. The Oneness of all creation
is shown in the unity of God and Christ.
"I and my Father are one…   (John 10:30, 38)
If you had known me,
you would also have known God."
And, "He who has seen me   (John 14:7-10)
has seen the Father."
This unity extends to us, too.
"You will know that I am in my Father,
and you in me, and I in you."
We are all interconnected.   (John 17:21-23)
We are united as a close family.

3. Jesus did not come to change
God's mind about humans –
God's love and mercy were everlasting
before time, and will be on into eternity.
But Jesus *did* come to us to change
our minds about God.
Jesus came to show us what God is like.
God desires healing and reconciliation;
not punishment and retribution.
God is love everlasting.
God desires a deep, personal relationship
with each and every person
regardless of who they are
or what they may have done.

4. Jesus did not come to judge the world,
but to save us from ourselves.
He taught about equality and equity;
he taught about humility and mercy;
he taught about seeing deeply into the heart;
he taught about forgiveness
and understanding.
Jesus said,
"I give you peace; not as the world gives,
but as God gives." (John 14:27)
"Let not your hearts be troubled;
believe in God, believe also in me."
"Love one another as I have loved you."
(John 15:12,17)

5. Jesus said, "Follow me."
If we decide to follow Jesus,
then we are joining with the down-trodden,
and with the outcasts,
and with the poor,
and with the lonely,
and with sinners...
So, how do we do this in our own lives?

6. We respond by seeking our true self,
and nurturing it in community.
We respond by imitating Christ
in our own unique way,
the way in which we were made
by the hand of God.
We respond by beginning at the place
where we are now,
and moving forward
just one moment at a time.

7. Even if we have chosen to follow Jesus,
even if we "got Jesus" on a specific date,
we do not become flawless angels.
We continue to make mistakes,
we continue to battle temptations,
we continue to fall short of God's Glory.
But God still loves us anyway.

8. Live to the fullest with the assurance
that Jesus walks with us,
embraced in the faith
that life will be fruitful
through his love and guidance.

9. We walk with Jesus on the journey
from our head to our heart,
knowing that each step rests
in enduring love, grace and mercy.
Because we can't do it alone,
even with all our spiritual discipline,
and all our sacrifices and self-denial.

10. We study the Gospels.
We try to see things as Jesus saw them –
united, interconnected, interdependent.
We try to say things that Jesus said –
"You are loved." "Peace be unto you."
We try to understand the way Jesus did –
in compassion, patience, and wisdom.
Life is love, and is the fullest
when it is expressed in our own way,
as it's needed in the present moment.
For Jesus taught us to pray,
"Thy kingdom come, Thy will be done,
On earth as it is in heaven." (Matt. 6:10)

3. THE HOLY SPIRIT AND US

1. God loves us so much (1 John 4:13)
that we were given the Holy Advocate
to teach us, and guide us, (John 14:26; 15:26; 16:13)
to comfort us, and
to sustain us in life.
The Spirit abides in each
and every person. (Luke 1:40-41)

2. Paul wrote, "The Holy Spirit is the power
that brings the soul to life. (Eph. 3:16-17)
It is the energy
that drives every one of us.
It is the breath of life
that lets us be
who we were meant to be."
The Holy Spirit is the outpouring
of God's love
over all time and in every place.

3. A farmer plants a seed (Mark 4:26-29)
where it can grow,
but the farmer can't make it grow.
It grows by the power of the Spirit.
The farmer has faith that it will grow
even though the farmer
may never see the harvest. (Romans 8)

4. We offer an act of love,
like planting a seed,
but we can't make it grow.
We place this offering
into the hands of God
and have faith that it will produce
what God wants it to produce
by the power of the Holy Spirit.

5. We are to love our neighbors as ourselves,
without expectation of a result,
without expectation of a return,
without any expectation of gain at all.
It is God's place, not ours,
to take this act of love
and grow it through the Holy Spirit.
Do the love, then let God grow it.

6. Our other task is to listen, listen, listen
to the guidance and wisdom
of the Holy Spirit   (Matt. 10:16-20)
in the stillness of the night,
in the stillness of our prayers.   (Ps. 51:6)
To be filled with the Holy Spirit
Is to be filled with the love of Christ.

"The Holy Spirit graciously breathes into us the gifts that lead to eternal life."   - Julian of Norwich

4. COMMUNITY

1. We are all part of a community;
a web of relationships   (Eph. 4:4-6, 11-16)
that have some common bond
which creates a sense
of identity and unity:
families, work groups, churches,
neighborhoods, towns, and
the Community of the Gospel.

2. These are the places where we try
to bring God's kingdom to earth
in service to others;
to unite all peoples
under the love and wisdom
of Our Lord.

RELATIONSHIPS

3. The lifeblood of any Community
is the love of God that flows through
the veins of relationships.
God is love itself;   (1 John 4)
The deeper and more honest
the relationship,
the more evident will be the love of God.

4. We receive each person
in our Community
with thankfulness and openness
knowing that they, too, are temples of God,
fellow travelers on the journey.
What can we do to help each other
along the way?   (1 Corinth. 3:16)

5. The flow of God's love
depends on how ready we are
to listen, receive, share,
and be vulnerable
in the image of Christ.
It depends on how willing we are
to put the good of the kingdom
above self-interests;
to let our false-self egos die,
and to grow in spirit,
that others may live.

6. Learn the stories of others;
take an interest in their well-being
with respect, dignity, and equity.
Love as we would be loved.
If one member suffers,   (1 Corinth. 12:26)
all suffer together with that member;
If one member is honored,
all rejoice together with that member.

7. We are all broken in some way,
in need of the love, healing
and support of Christ.
We affirm each other's potential
as beloved children of God,
growing and learning from the gifts
of each present moment.

8. There are people in the community
who suffer under a sense of guilt and hurt;
they need reassurance of God's Grace
and unconditional love.
They can return to God's family;
to a place they actually never left.
None of God's children will be lost
in the final gathering – none.

DIVERSITY

9. We become fuller and more complete
as we tap into different relationships
built on God's love.
Strength in diversity
builds strength in community.
As Paul writes, "There is a variety of gifts,
services, and activities among us,
but we all have   (1 Corinth.12)
the same Spirit, Lord and God
for the common good.

10. Just as the body has many members,
it is still one body;   (John 10:16)
so it is with the body of Christ
of which we are all a part.
One member of the body
is no less important than another;
what good is it if we are all alike?"

11. Because we all have one Creator,
we are all brothers and sisters
even though we are all unique.
No better, no worse – just unique.
God loves each of the children
very deeply, and very personally.
So, too, must we love.

12. This is the whole reason
we exist as a Community –
to know, love, and serve God
in our own unique way,
based on the specific talents,
skills, and interests
that we have been given.

LEADERSHIP

13. Jesus is the only perfect leader;
the head of the Church.
The Church is all of God's *people*;
Not just buildings.
The Church has many groups
which have leaders,
but all must follow Christ.
He has placed them there
to care and nurture
the members of the group.

14. While the leaders need authority,
they should not be authoritarians.
While they must be heard,
they must also listen.
While they must be loved,
they must also be loving.
While we are accountable to them;
they are accountable to God,
and to us,
for their leadership.

15. Together we seek
the building up of all our members,
of kindred souls,
to make the community whole
by growing in the love of the Lord.

Pray for the leaders,
and for those who follow,
let us be leaders in our own way,
the way we were made to be.

*"If we have no peace, it is because we have forgotten
that we belong to each other."*
- Mother Teresa

5. BEING HUMAN

1. The creation story tells us that
God formed people from the earth,
and breathed into their nostrils
the breath of life;
and they became living beings.
People were created in God's image,
according to God's likeness.
And God called this "good."
So we, too, should call it good
and begin our understanding of people
as a blessing, and not a curse.
Our inherent identity stems
from the very life of God.

2. The core of our identity,
our actual being and soul,
is sometimes referred to
as the True Self.   (Romans 7:20)
It knows who we really are.
It is connected to
all the other True Selves
in the world, and to God.
Because of this,
we are all interrelated
and interdependent.

3. We sometimes forget this and get lost.
We forget that we came
with a built-in connection to our Creator,
a love-line from God's heart to ours.
We somehow get separated from God,
at least in our minds, but not in God's mind.
Then we try to find our identity
in many of the wrong things
instead of in God.
Paul tells us that
one of our main challenges in life
is to reconnect to our original identity
"hidden with Christ in God."   (Colossians 8:3)
Perhaps this is one way of defining salvation.

4. A false self can emerge from within,
a "little self" that tries to confuse us
with illusions, and tempts us with power,
or prejudice, or fear, or busy-ness.
It feeds on guilt and shame,
on anxiety and arrogance.
We must be aware when this happens,
and pause to check on reality.
We must seek the inner true self
with prayer, meditation and contemplation,
and finding God in the patterns of life
that we see around us.

5. To dissolve the false self
should not be a violent act.
We simply work to become aware of it
and all the waste
and harm it can cause us.
Soon, the scales over our eyes fall away
and we begin to see clearly, deeply.
We die to the old self,   (Acts 9:17-19)
that our new self may live.
We empty ourselves of the old,
to make room for the new.

6. The fruits of the Spirit shine through,
and we gradually begin to know
who we are – our interests,
our skills, our likes,
and how we are interconnected
to those around us.
We gradually become
who we were made to be,
not anything we want to be,
but who we are supposed to be.
That's all we are,
and that's more than enough.

7. We are a blend of calm and chaos,
darkness and light, pain and pleasure;
But God loves us as we are anyway.

We experience the Gospel of Grace
when we accept that we are accepted,
and loved.

8. In our True Self
we begin to see ourselves
and others deeply.   (John 7:24)
We see past false selves and   (1 Sam. 16:7)
into the depths of the human heart.
We see possibilities and bridges,
where before we saw
only limits and walls.
We no longer think in "either/or" terms,
but rather we think in "and/also" terms.

9. Instead of division, we see unity.
Instead of separation, we see connection.
Instead of competition, we see collaboration.
Instead of scarcity, we see abundance.
Instead of privilege, we see fairness.
Instead of blame, we see forgiveness.
Instead of punishment, we see restoration.
Instead of hurting, we see healing.
Instead of falsehood, we see truth.
Instead of death, we see life.

"My Grace is enough for you: My power is at its
best in your weakness."   (2 Corinth. 12:9)

6. THE GOOD NEWS
The Holy Gospel

1. In the Gospel
we discover the Good News:
God so loved the world
that God gave the Son,   (John 3:16, 17)
and whosoever believed in him
would not perish, but have everlasting life.
For God did not send the Son
to condemn the world, but to save it.

2. God's love for us is pure and everlasting;
it is unconditional and boundless.
We learn that there is nothing – nothing –
that can come between us
and God's love for us.   (Romans 8:38-39)
There is no power strong enough,
no evil bad enough,
no devil big enough;
even we, ourselves,
can't separate God's love from us.

3. God wants us to know
that God understands
that our world is a difficult
and dangerous place to live,
and that it is not easy to live here.

But we should also know
that we are assured a place
in the Kingdom nonetheless.
This is the Good News – we're guaranteed
a place through God's Grace.

4. God came to us in a form
we might understand.
God showed us that the material
and the spiritual can unite
and be as One.
God sent Jesus in God's Name,
to teach us, and heal us, and show us
how to live together.
Not to let our true selves die
under the burden of illusion or false gods,
but have the life that was breathed into us
from the beginning.
The good news of the Gospel
is that we can discover the eternal life
in Jesus' life and ministry.
Jesus is the model for each person
and the community as a whole.

5. Jesus came and said, "Follow me."
An invitation which can be accepted,
or can be rejected.

Because love requires free will
we are always given choices.
Once we begin the journey
we may fall now and then,
but the invitation still stands, forever.
Always get up, knowing that we fall,
it's on a bed of mercy and forgiveness.
We are set aright once again
by the power and love of the Holy Spirit.

6. To follow Jesus means
we need to be empty of ourselves,
ready to receive what he has to offer.
It means allowing the heart connections
with people, and with nature, to grow.
It means learning to see deeply,
past our own shortcomings,
and past those of others,
to look into the hearts of life everywhere.
It means to listen to the words of others,
and to listen for what has not been said,
to reach people at their point of need.
We work to allow dignity for all,
building respect and ensuring equality.

7. To follow Jesus binds us to his Word,
but also releases us
from the bondage of pride,
power, privilege, prejudice,
and other false gods.
We no longer have to justify our choices,
because our guidance
comes from the Holy Spirit –
to love, share, and care as Jesus did.
Our path has already been selected –
to follow the love and life of Christ.

8. We use the Gospel as the reason
for our vow of Prayer;
we use the Gospel as the resource
for our vow of Study;
we use the Gospel as the example
for our vow of Service.
Let us fill our minds and hearts
with the love of Christ
through the Gospel every day,
morning and evening,
and every moment in between.

> *"Always preach the Gospel,*
> *and if necessary, use words."*
>   - Attributed to St. Francis

7. THE BREAD OF LIFE
The Eucharist

1. Jesus said,
"I am the bread of life; (John 6:35)
anyone who comes to me
shall not hunger,
and who believes in me
shall never thirst"
This bread and living water is from God,
and comes down from heaven
to give life to the world.

2. There is no true life
without the Presence of God.
There is no true life
without the incarnate God
present in the flesh of Christ.
So when we eat the bread,
and drink from the cup,
we are receiving
the love of Christ
inside of us, incarnate.
He abides in us,
and we in him.
We become all one family.

3. The Eucharistic meal
should not define who is a member
of the Church, and who is not,
but should instead
proclaim the gift of grace
to all people.
A meal together
removes all the things
that might separate
one people from another.
When we eat together,
we become one, in Christ.

4. Jesus is the food,
and all we have to do
is to provide the hunger.
But all too often
we are already full of ourselves,
our ideas, our idols, our righteousness;
so, we are not hungry.
To be hungry, we have to be empty.
We must come to the table
willing to receive,
to make room for divine Presence,
and accept unconditionally
the love that is offered
unconditionally for all.

5. But what is it
that gives this body life?
What nourishes us to keep us healthy?
It is the blood of Christ
that flows through the veins
of relationships.
"Drink this, all of you,   (Matt. 26)
as a testament for my love for you."
For what greater love
does anyone have,
than to lay down his life for another?
The Cup makes us truly
all one holy family.
We join in a common heart
with a common purpose
that is fulfilled in our own unique ways.

6. The core of our life
is the celebration of the Eucharist;
and we celebrate it at the Holy Table,
and in every encounter,
and in every moment in life.
So, we never actually leave the Holy Table.
We are there when we help the poor,
or clothe the needy, or give thanks,
or appreciate nature,
or when we just listen to another person.

7. If we lose sight of this,
like the two traveling   (Luke 24:13-35)
on the road near Emmaus,
our hearts can grow heavy.
But when we come back to the Table,
Jesus will once again
be made known to us
by the breaking of the Bread.

8. The Last Supper was, in reality,
the First Supper –
one of many that will continue forever.
It was not a farewell meal,
but a model of how to live with,
and love each other.
The gifts of God,
for the people of God.
Take them in remembrance
that Christ lived for you,
and feed on him in your hearts
by faith, with thanksgiving.
"Do this... in remembrance of me."

"There are so many hungry people in the world that God could only come into the world in the form of food." - Gandhi

8. THE BODY OF CHRIST
The Church

1. The Church emerged over time
through the inspiration
of the Holy Spirit
to further God's kingdom on earth.
It is not so much the buildings,
or the dogmas,
or the creeds,
as it is the people
bound together in the love of Christ.

2. Jesus left no specific instructions
about how to create a Church,
other than to love our neighbors
as ourselves.
This love is the basic value
from which the institution would grow,
despite its faults,
and issues,
and failings over time.
Our love for the Church
should be expressed
in a union of faith with Jesus
as taught in the Gospels.

3. The Church must do what Jesus did:
include the excluded,
heal the sick,
strengthen the weak,
love the despised,
clothe the naked,
ensure economic equity,
seek restorative justice,
respect and replenish nature,
and insist that those in power
use their influence
to do the same.
This does not require
supernatural powers,
but it does require commitment.

4. We are all imperfect
and fall short of God's glory.
But this is not something
to be condemned.
Instead we must affirm our potential,
and focus on our original blessing
that what God created is "good."
Salvation is a journey
to spiritual maturity
with the help of the Church.

5. The Church has the charge
to seek reconciliation,
and not to condemn.
We, the Church, must try
to seek to understand,
more than to be understood.
Seek to see deeply,
more than to be seen.
Seek to hear,
more than to be heard.
Seek to give,
more than to be given to.
Seek to help,
more than to be helped.
In helping others,
we help ourselves.

6. Our understanding
and awareness of God
grows over time.
Let the Church be flexible
to accept change
without compromising
the basic value of love.
Never let doctrine
interfere with grace.
The Church is a means,
and not the end.

7. To love Christ
is to love the Church.
Wherever two or more people
are gathered in his Name,
we have the organized Church.
When we are with someone else,
that place is holy and sacred.
It is a relationship;
a vehicle of faith, hope, and love;
a potential place of peace
that passes all understanding;
a place where the kingdom of heaven
touches the earth.

> *"Our soul will never find rest until it unites with
> Jesus and understands that he is the fullness of all
> joy."* - Julian of Norwich

9. PRAYER

1. Although God is always with us,
prayer is when we are most conscious of it.
Prayer is time spent with God,
where we are empty and open,
ready to receive whatever is offered,
ready to give whatever needs to be given.
It means being present to the moment,
acknowledging the God in us, and us in God,
where the divine being and the human being
come together as one.

2. What we do in prayer, and how we do it,
depends a lot on who we are.
It's often shaped by our personality.
It can be formal or informal,
it can be silent or with words,
it can be short or long,
it can be structured or spontaneous,
it can be done alone, in secret,
or when we're in Community with others.
It can be with music, or candles,
or incense, or books,
it can be for ourselves or for the world,
it can be for telling God something,
or for just listening to God.
Prayer can even be a walk in the woods,
or sitting with our pets.

3. We pray for different reasons,
but they're all good reasons.
Sometimes we want to give thanks,
sometimes we need something for ourselves,
sometimes we are asking for others,
but sometimes we just want
to sit alone with God,
to be present with God,
and bask in the steadfast love
being offered to us.

4. Sometimes we just don't know
what to say, or how to say it.
And that's when we must let
the Holy Spirit speak for us.
It may not even be spoken in words,
but in images or feelings,
because words are often not enough.

5. Prayer usually leaves us
changed in some way.
Other things around us
may not change,
God may not change,
our problems may not change,
but the way we understand them
may change.
And that newness sometimes makes
all the difference in the world...

A fresh approach to action
may be realized,
or we may reconcile
to accept what is.

6. Prayer is the cornerstone of our vocation.
The path to knowing God
is to know our own soul more.
The path to knowing our own soul
is to know God more.
The path to each is prayer.
The more we live in each moment,
the more we will find ourselves
in a state of prayer.
Prayer will blend into service
and into study,
and the three will be hard to tell apart.
And that's the way it should be.

7. Prayer is the breath of life.
Inhaling, we receive God's presence,
love, wisdom, comfort, understanding,
and healing as a gift.
Exhaling, we share this love
in renewal with others as a new self.
It is by this that God will be glorified.

10. SERVICE
Helping Others

1. All forms of service are rooted
in the Lord's Prayer when we pray
"Thy Kingdom come, Thy will be done,
on Earth as it is in heaven."   (Matt. 6:9-13)
Jesus is telling us that heaven
should not only be thought of
as someplace off in the future,
but that it should also be happening
right now, here on Earth.
And God wants us to be involved
in making it happen.

2. Heaven is like the sum total
of all the bits and pieces of love
that occur in every moment,
in every place,
revealing the presence of God.
Another word for service is, in fact, "love."
"By this all will know that you are my disciples,
if you have love for one another."   (John 13:35)
If you are the wisest person,
the smartest person,
the most accomplished person,
or the wealthiest person,
but have not love,
then you are nothing.   (1 Corinth. 13:1-3)

3. We look to the Beatitudes
as the model for our service,
the framework upon which
to bring heaven to Earth.   (Matt. 5:1-12)
We strive to be "poor in spirit,"
emptying ourselves of anything
that is not of God – allowing
our true selves to emerge.
We mourn, showing our sensitivity
and awareness for the plight
of others and for the world;
We seek humility, understanding that
our place with God is no higher, or lower,
than anyone else.   (Luke 14:7-11)

4. We pursue righteousness, which is
restorative justice in all political,
social, and economic systems.
That means that all people are respected,
loved, and treated with dignity.
Do not forget the person in front of you
while you confront the bigger issue far off.
The passion for an issue
may cause you to love the issue
more than the person it affects.

5. We seek peace among all peoples,
which is based on the pursuit
of restorative justice, mercy,
and a deeper understanding of each other.
And we know that sometimes
helping other people in mankind's world,
we may place ourselves in the path of
ridicule, derision, and danger.
But since we walk the path of Christ,
we are fed by his joy and love.

6. And what of the big issues around the
world? What can we possibly do?
First, we must understand
what causes these problems.
The answer: almost everything causes them!
Everything is the cause,
because in reality everything
is connected with everything else.
Some connections are direct and obvious,
and others are very subtle and uncertain.
But they are all very real.
Science is gradually discovering
what the world's great religions
have known for millennia –
that everything is connected to everything.

7. So, if everything is interconnected,
then some of those connections
must be right there in front of us,
within our grasp.
We can influence even the biggest
of problems and begin to change them,
even if only in some small way.
Every positive thought,
every well-spoken word,
every small act of kindness
whether it is witnessed or not,
will ripple out and find its way
through the grand circuitry of life
and begin to make changes for the better.

8. Jesus said, "Even if you do something
for the least of these,
you do it for me."   (Matthew 25:40)
Never underestimate the little things.
Together we can move mountains!
So we use our unique talents,
skills, and interests,
whatever they happen to be,
and we look around us,
for opportunities in the moment
to be of service to God in love.
Any act of love – however large or small –
is of the greatest importance to God.
It's God Grace that brings the results.

9. We do the act of love,
and then we let the Holy Spirit take over
to do with it as the Spirit desires.
The foundation of our service rests on
our love for God, our neighbors,
and ourselves,   (Matt. 22:37-40)
as the Great Commandment dictates.
We do what we can with what
we have been given, and in the place
where we have been planted.
Our efforts are based in truth,
and are non-violent to others,
to the world, and to ourselves.
Violence is always costly
and the hurt doesn't always heal.

10. And let us not forget the service
we need for ourselves, too,
for Jesus said to love God,
and our neighbors, *as ourselves*.
We claim the refreshing pauses we need
from our outward service
to ensure sufficient care
for our inward needs.
Rest as Jesus did,
and then return to the tasks at hand.
Honor the Sabbath rest.

11. CREATION

1. In the beginning,
God created the heavens   (Gen. 1:1)
and the earth,
through the Word.   (John 1:1-3)
For in the beginning was the Word,
and the Word was with God,
and the Word was God.
All things were made by the Word,
and nothing was made without him.

2. The stars were made by the Word,
the earth was made by the Word,
the birds were made by the Word,
the trees were made by the Word;
the seashells and sand,
the oceans and puddles,
the ants and behemoths,
the wind and clouds,
and us.

3. And God, with the Word,
sat back and rested,   (Gen. 1:31)
and looked at all They had made,
and They called it "good."   (Eph. 2:10)

4. God's love for creation
and for us
could not be contained.
It swirled around within the Trinity,
and then poured forth into creation.
God's love is evident   (Rom. 1:20)
in all the things that have been made.
God's love is unconditional   (Rom. 8:38-39)
and has always been that way.

5. We cannot exist
without nature;
nature is not complete
without us.
There is an abundance for all
in nature's gifts,
if they are used properly.
We accept these gifts
as we need,
not as we want,
and we share so that all people
have their needs met.
And we work to replenish the gifts
we have been given.
For we own nothing of it,
but we are caretakers of it all.

6. If we lose our connection with nature,
we lose our connection with God.
Our busy-ness in this world
blinds us to God's world around us.
We forget that the world
is full of God's Grace,
revealed in spirit and in matter:
rainbows, clouds, and rain,
music, birds, and children playing.
God reminds us of this Grace
in all that is good.

7. We are called to be co-creators with God,
to express our love
in many and diverse forms.
So, create some good,
create some art,
create lots of love.
Receive gratefully
and give back joyfully.

8. The pattern of God
is found in all things.
To know all things
we must first learn to deeply know
the thing before us,
the person before us,
or the creature before us,
in the present moment, right now.

9. To say we love humanity,
we must be able to love the person
in front of us.   (1 Corin. 13:1-3)
Love is more important than intellect,
understanding, or knowledge.
To express this love,
we begin with a small act of kindness
to each and every person we meet,
every creature we encounter,
and every bit of nature we experience.
It could very well be that
these small acts of kindness
are the very things that save the world.
And they're actually quite easy to do.

12. WORLDLY THINGS

1. "All things came into being through him;
and without him not
one thing came into being."   (John 1:3)
The sun, moon, and stars,
and all the elements within,
were made by the Word,
out of God's love.

2. From these gifts, mankind's creativity has
discovered and invented
wondrous things.
But mankind's spiritual growth suffered
under the weight of this inventiveness.
The efficiencies and luxuries of life
captured the hearts of the privileged,
creating inequity in economics,
politics, social structures,
and the use of nature's bounty.
The love of money, power, and prestige
infected the human mind,
creating false gods
and growing scales of illusion
over the eyes that lit the soul.
"You shall worship the Lord your God,
and Him only shall you serve."   (Matt. 4:10)

3. Our challenge is to lay up treasures
for ourselves in the vault of heaven.
These are harder to see,
harder to believe in,
and cannot be gathered directly.
They come to our account
through the imitation of Christ –
by bearing his Word
in the presence of love
each moment in time.
They begin where our heart is –
the product of God's love in us –
then shine forth into the world.

4. A true heart seeks
a right attitude and approach
to worldly things
without renouncing the gifts of God.
We use what we have been given
in the service of others,
seeking dignity, respect and equity
for all persons.
And we receive gratefully
those things we are in need of,
offering thankfulness for these gifts.

5. Know well the lesson
of the vineyard workers: (Matt. 20:1-16)
In God's eyes, all people deserve
the minimum needed to live decently;
not based on merit,
or connections,
or talent, or opportunities,
or ethnicity –
but because they are children of God.
If we have more than we need,
we watch for opportunities
to share the excess   (Luke 3:11)
with those truly in need.

6. We endeavor to replenish
what we receive from the earth,
being ever mindful
of the earth's precious resources.
We endeavor to distinguish
between a need and a want,
knowing that our minds will sometimes
confuse the two.
We endeavor to emotionally detach
from all worldly things,
because it is impossible
to serve two masters.   (Luke 16:13)

7. Jesus said, "Take heed   (Luke 12:15)
and beware of covetousness –
for a person's life does not consist
in the abundance of things possessed."
We are not nourished
by the things of this world,
but by every word   (Matt.4)
that is uttered from the heart of God.

8. We walk carefully
as sheep among wolves
when we interact with the rich or powerful
who may be blinded by various delusions.
We gird ourselves with love and patience,
and strengthen our resolve,
knowing that the Holy Advocate
will guide us unto a path of peace
while we persist in a quest
to live the Gospel
through the prayer, study and service
of our vocations.

*"Seek first the Kingdom of God and its righteousness,
and all these things will be added unto you." (Matt. 6:33)*

13. MARY
An Example for Living

1. Favored by God,   (Luke 1:26-38)
Mary became the vessel
by which the gift
of the Incarnation was given.
What can we all learn
from her life of love?

2. Mary showed us humility
when the angel greeted her
as the "favored one."
She was perplexed by the words
and pondered their meaning.
She was empty of self-pride,
ready to be the place
where God and human become one.
"The Mighty One has done great things for
me, and holy is His name."   (Luke1:49)

3. The Magi traveled far
to offer their gifts to the holy family,
bringing with them wise words and prophecy
concerning the Christ child.   (Matt. 2:1-12)
All who heard it were amazed,
but Mary treasured all these words
and pondered them in her heart.

4. The uncertain future of this child
was wrapped with Mary's faith and trust
in God's providence.
May we also have this strength of heart
as we walk into the unknown.

5. She watched her child grow
in strength and knowledge of the Lord.
He has scattered the proud,   (Luke 1:51)
he has brought down the powerful,
he has lifted up the lowly,
he has filled the hungry,
he has healed and taught in love.

6. She knew the dangers facing her child,
but she remained steadfast
in her devotion to him,
even unto death on the cross.
Through despair and suffering,
through separation and helplessness,
she remained assured that this divine Light
would not be extinguished.

7. Mary was first to give birth to Jesus;
She gave the Christ child to the world.
We, too, can give birth to this Son of God!
Let him come forth
from the depths of our hearts,

and enter our own lives,
not only to help others through us,
but to walk with us in our joys,
and support us in our struggles.

8. Let us respond as Mary did
when she was called to service,
humbly, openly, and joyfully:
"Here am I, servant of the Lord;   (Luke 1:38)
Let it be unto me according to your word."

14. LIVING NOW
The Present Moment - Mindfulness

1. We come from the past,
and are headed to the future,
but we do not belong in either place.
We only truly live in each moment
between the past and the future.
Each one of those moments
contains all the riches of God's kingdom.

2. As we walk our spiritual journey,
every single step we take
is being in the present moment.
Not the last step we took,
or the one we are about to take,
but the one right now.
Everything real that happens to us
happens in the present moment.
All else is an illusion.

3. Our connection with God
only occurs in the present.
God's love can only be shared
in the present moment.
Our presence in the present moment
links us into the field of all possibilities;
it's where we connect with others,
allowing our prayer power to flow out,

and where we receive
the flow of love and blessings.
The precious present is ours.

4. What happens to us in the present moment
are the very circumstances that show us
which way to go, and give us
the opportunity to practice kindness,
and patience, and love.
Instead of trying to control
what circumstances enter our life,
we manage what our responses will be
to the things as they occur.

5. Living in the present moment
does not mean we forget the past
or ignore the future.
What it means is that we use
the past and the future
in the proper way.
They can become debilitating baggage
or benevolent gifts.

6. Our past experiences are teachers,
and we must learn from them.
But we avoid dwelling on them
to the point that they interfere
with our present moment.

7. Planning for the future is helpful,
but living there is not.   (Matt. 6:34)
So, plan if we must,
but come back home
to the present moment.
The steps to the future
all happen in the present moment,
one at a time.
Now is when the future is made.

8. The present moment is the place
where life's big decisions are made.
The deepest of these is whether
we choose to follow God
or the devilish dysfunctions of our ego.
No matter how far we are on the journey,
this challenge never ends.
Sometimes we choose God,
and sometimes we do not.

9. Our best choices are made
when we are most aware of ourselves.
To do this, our minds, bodies, and spirits
must all be in the moment first.
We become the observer of our thoughts
and how we're spending our time.
We become more aware
of the physical world around us –
we use our five senses with intention.

10. This awareness is helped by
paying attention to our own breathing,
or feeling the movement as we walk,
or watching the flight of a bird,
or seeing all the shades of a color
where before we thought we saw only one.
Listen for the voice of God in the breeze,
and in the words of another person.
Feel the grass or the leaf of a plant.
Treat objects as gifts of God.
Look at people as temples of God.
Consider each of your movements
as a sacrament to God.

11. Present moment awareness
is the key to living a full life.
It's the essence of being.
The present moment
is the only period of time
when we are truly conscious.

12. To discover the Kingdom
is the easiest thing in the world
because the Kingdom
is all around us
and within us.
But it is difficult to possess,
because it only exists
in the present moment,

and because to possess it
means we must possess nothing else.
The more we let go of ourselves,
the more we come to realize this.

13. Let us leave the past to God's mercy,
and the future to God's providence,
and seek God's Kingdom
in the present moment.

*"What does it matter, Lord, if the future is bleak! I
cannot pray for tomorrow's needs...keep my heart
pure, keep me in your shade, just for today."*
                                        - St. Therese of Lisieux

15. THE SPIRITUAL JOURNEY

1. The desire to travel the spiritual road
from our head to our heart
is deeply embedded in the fiber of our soul.
This desire is created by God,
assured by the Son,
sustained by the Holy Spirit,
and is fueled by the love of God.

2. Sacred words throughout the world,
and over many millennia,
describe a three-fold response
to this desire for unity with God:
The Way of Devotion,
which has become our vow of Prayer;
The Way of Knowledge,
which has become our vow of Study;
And the Way of Action,
which has become our vow of Service.

3. But these ways are not the end,
they are only the means to get there.
But where is there?
It is to be united with God,
in our hearts, and our minds,
and our bodies.

4. These vows were not meant to be burdens,
but rather the blessings of nourishment
that are needed to keep us going.
They will lighten our paths
and reveal the Kingdom of God
all around us and in us.

5. Our journey becomes ever lighter
as we leave things behind along the way.
At one point we may surrender pride,
and at another we surrender the false self.
Later we may begin to share privileges,
and gradually we drop anything
that causes our separation from others.
These are the scales that must be shed
for reconciliation to blossom,
for salvation to show its way,
and for peace to make its home with us.

6. Jesus said that unless we become
like little children, we will never be able
to see or understand   (Matt. 18:2-4)
the Kingdom of Heaven.
We must be willing to accept ourselves;
to empty ourselves of ego;
to be a part of the community
and not the center of it;
To be open-minded, curious, and in awe.

7. Our attention may be on each step
of the trail, our eyes pointing downward.
But footsteps of others can still be heard;
because we don't travel alone.
We can't travel alone –
because we can't do it alone.
God within us, and Christ by our side,
and companions all around.
We grow in gentleness and strength
within this nest of hearts
as we nourish each other's souls
along the way.

8. And as we walk this road through life,
like the two on the road to Emmaus,
we never forget to break the bread of life.
It renews our strength and purpose,
but more importantly it reminds us that we
are in the Presence of God
whenever we are with another person,
or creature, or cloud,   (Luke 24:13-35)
or even when we're alone.

9. We ride each moment through time,
seeing so many changes
through the windows of our eyes.
So much that once was,
but is no longer.
People we knew are gone,
and new ones enter our lives.

We feel like grasping for handles,
anything to hang on to,
but most slip past,
leaving only images in unsettled memory.
What is real? What is illusion?
What can be trusted?
Jesus said, "I am the way,
and the truth, and the life." (John 14:6)

10. The road ahead has hills and valleys;
there are dark places and dry places.
Some of our lives here on earth
just don't end well.
Sometimes our lives stay wet with tears,
and we are left to wonder why.
But each drop is sacred,
and will be remembered,
and will be reconciled.

11. Wherever we are, so is God –
The Lord is our shepherd,
helping us to find the still waters
and green pastures.
For his goodness and mercy will follow us
all the days of our lives,
and we shall dwell
in the House of the Lord forever. (Psalm 23)

12. We are on a journey without end.
When this life ends, another begins.
There's more – there's always more.
God's unconditional love for us
does not change when we pass
from this life into the next.
We are all bound for a place
at Christ's Table in the Kingdom ahead,
where the sign over the gate will read,
"Welcome Home."

His disciples said, "Yes, now you are speaking plainly,
not in any figure of speech! Now we know that you
know all things, and do not need to have anyone
question you; by this we believe that you came from
God."
(John 16:29-30)

Suggested Reading Plan

Try reflecting on a chapter a day!
Read chapter 1 on the first day of the month,
and then read chapter 2 on day 2, and so on.
Beginning on the 16th of the month,
start over again with chapter 1.
Make changes to your Personal Rule of Life
and your Journal as needed, based on the
reflections from each day.

The Community of the Gospel is a dispersed monastic Community in North America, where we help each other discover Christ in our lives. Although we live and work in different places, we are united by God's love, and strive to build a common monastic practice based on Daily Prayer, Reflective Study and Personal Service – common roots that lead to unique responses to God's love in our lives.

www.communityofthegospel.org

Made in the USA
Monee, IL
26 May 2020